Moon Wrasse

Willo Drummond

PUNCHER & WATTMANN

First published in 2023
Published by Puncher & Wattmann
PO Box 279
Waratah NSW 2298

info@puncherandwattmann.com

NATIONAL
LIBRARY
OF AUSTRALIA

A catologue record for this book is available from The National Library of Australia.

ISBN   9781922571670

Cover design by Miranda Douglas

Section illustrations by Adam Byatt

Printed by Lightning Source International

This project has been assisted by the Australian Government through the Australia Council, its arts funding and advisory body.

Australian Government

Australia | Council
for the Arts

Contents

Arriving

Seed

At this season's out-welling
after the mangrove moon
she sets her grief in a small seed pod

sends it out across the river.
In waning luminescence
on the aqua-terrestrial shore

she trains her eye
to velvet vivipary
on very salty water.

She's looking for
a future
to enframe the past

as it exceeds
it. Flickering familiar
like the pulse

of being needed.
Here in the interstitial
here in the lyric tense

she stills to witness
each furred pod
gain its wild purpose—

her perfect body weightless
as flesh and thought are freed
where *what cannot be*

is
and is
and so must be.

The art of losing

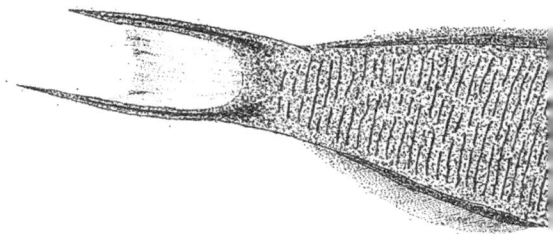

The act of making

after Louise Glück's 'Love Poem' and 'The Wild Iris'

'There is always something to be made
of pain,' she said. A claret scarf. A soufflé. Misshapen

gardens fecund with memory and fluffed
intentions. How can you bear

so many imagined blooms heavy with scent of hope
let go? You tend tender

shoots, day after day, while remembrance
scratches your knuckles, and solitary bees

hover, uncertain what to make
of such circuitous traversing

of stiff dry earth. Unwomanly. Bent queen
brimful of ~~love~~ shame with nowhere to dig

in. You strike, scrape flushed clay seeking
signs. Portents.   Why

the seasons unfolded as they did. Why
the iris falls blue as the moon.   Why

cicadas go on singing, when song hushed
long ago in your throat. No one can say. Parched

you shake barren dust
from boots, walk on

and on to build another bed
simply for the act of making.

Somewhere, a ghost orchid blooms.

Up to our knees in it

We're up to our knees
in it, here on the flats
our feet
constantly wet.

Black rims our edges
as we extrude reason, baking
on decks in seasons
new minted
while past the 'no fishing' sign
down at the front
cinema seats and soft drink
cans get down and dirty
with the kids.

These kids can live anywhere,
beneath the hum of the highway
a constant, keeping mute
like a consonant
that *suddenly stops the breath.*

Keep on running, sight-blind bound
living life at a precarious angle
living local like a canon on a slow drip feed

(the air is slightly sour
with it). No matter,
mangroves will take
our mishaps
down, turn them in
to bluest carbon.

And we'll keep dreaming
we're not sinking
as we strain toward the light.

Propagules for drift and dispersal

Avicennia marina has a viviparous seeding
habit. It keeps its babies close. Many mangrove

children—on departure from the coop—set sail
across the ocean, travel for months at sea. Weaker

avicennia though, don't stray very far. Seeds
often become stranded, establishing close to their parents.

When I was one such kid, I couldn't wait to flee
this drowned river valley. The scent of mud

in my pores, the cloying air, the constant presence
of swamp dwellers' stares. This wasn't the stand for me.

I wanted to be my own island, to gather
my people close. I wanted to open myself

to the world—of words, vaporous thoughts, gestures
like silk—at least to say triumphant: *mother, I've left*

your long body. Through sheer force of willpower
I'd build my own *terra firma*; show life was more than a sentence

-based rehearsal. But today, I read in the paper:
'the mangrove is probably the most remarkable

community of unrelated families in the world.'
So much for distant mangrove shores.

Trying not to let life ruffle my feathers, I consider
what time and tide has told me: slowly

the lines are silting over. One grabs

a whiff of a future though, if you massage the meaning
of mangrove. Even on an island, change is the surest

constant. There's always mud around the edges
and memories that slip through our fingers. We're all

sucking down carbon, and small shards of selves
keep protruding, for a micro-breath. Glimpse across

the saltpan as the tide edges in: you'll see you
can sail as far as you like, but you'll never leave

this station. So much is pneumataphoric metaphor
and urban, suburban, sub-sub-urban transpiration.

The children

after Vera Newsom's 'Sligo'

Through streaming trees
night birds hurtling
along electric river
torrents of mind:
that child, my children
they come. Spectral voices

ride each wave of foam
disperse in pools
of words like shards
of glass; every hue
tessellated in suggestive
geometry. As though

lives were quantities
more certain
than sand
castles, knowable as stone
houses, red roofs
at dawn, the comfort

of rising light.

Unspoken

This silent grief's
stigma, stems words'

line. Snuffs blooms
from heady night.

Texture of dry petals, friable
threads of vegetal

language. I trace each string
of particles unspoken, map

chambers of disenfranchised
song through hollow shell.

Walk, un-storied
ghost for life's quarter season;

pause: bloomless
epiphyte in unimagined

place, living on air—
fumes of hope

in the key of *someday, someday*—
still waiting for conditions

to align. / Watching the moon.

Ways of seeing

after Felicity Plunkett's 'Underwater Caulking'

One perigee syzygy, a poem speaks
of *the ten lunar months it takes / to make
a child.* In ancient Egypt

these intervals were understood
to begin when the waning
could no longer be seen

before first light. Currently
you are stardust.
Not even

              yet
a crescent.
I worry I've lost too many

hours waning. My knowing
too slim;
a left-aligned filament

that cannot catch
and hold
          a feather

let alone a ray
of shimmering dust. Perhaps, gibbous
with confusion, I'm spent?

(Will I, won't I? This way or that?)
While others turn with such precision,
radiant orbs—content

filled—I dream of conjunctions
luminous alignments
stackings of hope

in indigo night.
A matter of perspective, of course,
our nearness.

Glimmering illusion
that you are

so easily within   reach.

Sail

In an instant you are a sail
$\qquad\qquad$ loosed, flapping. Sprayed

with a sea of tiny blades—
a vast, over-sensate skin. Your silent

voice, a gaping mouth, calls
from a crack in the world: *desolate*

wind, sweep my knowledge
into oblivion, drop me back

in the well. All that sounds is the clink of flailing
shackles against the mast.

Experience says, in time,
$\qquad\qquad$ the canvas will snap

taut. Right now
this sheet is the shape of living.

The ladder's blown
the world's all wailing wind.

Archaeology

Through labyrinthine tunnels
we travel,
      blind

      feeling
along cool abutments, bracing
crumbling walls.

   The archaeology of grief
is an outfit tailored from stolen sky
a talisman fashioned from albatross wings

   unsuited for confinement.
It takes time upon time upon time again
but the canary is still singing

   (silver moon not yet lost
at bottom of silted well).
With rudimentary tools

   we follow the need
of two, an animal
art of bodies

   tunneling to something more.
Side by side, we sift
saturated sediment

   sand, rock, muck
all the earth of mind
we *weigh by carat of heart.*

We find blood, yes,
but also *glance and gesture*
forgotten ways of sight;

so when we reach the water table
on which our city floats
when we glimpse the rusted ladder that leads towards the light

we know to stow our picks and grasp with two hands, the frame
of each breaking, tenderskinned
ending, to the ink of night.

Some words for migratory birds

Remember last year on the flyway
just before the fourth stopover,
you taught me to read star-maps
under a blush of sea-sprayed moonlight

Direction was magnetic
then: I-you-she-he-we
moved shore-to-shore
without the burden of

knowing. Flying in tight
   formation, hearts
        driven with
           intention

[Now we witness the birth
of a white-bellied sea-eagle
on a two-inch screen]

My hand—my limb—reaches
for the familiar feel of your wingtip
while you, preoccupied, testing the waters
of transformation, almost miss the cue

Thing is, the slightest shift in alkalinity
sets the whole thing in motion. We must
conserve our energy, for there's just
so far to go. Here
                    listen to my voice:
                    the world is waiting for you

and your flight-notes. What
will you make of them?   Turn

face northward

embark—

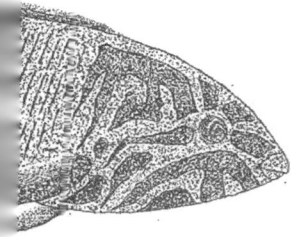

On finding and not finding Levertov

When words penetrate deep into us they change the chemistry of the soul,
of the imagination.
Denise Levertov, 'The Poet in the World'

The Levadeiro

On the Island of Madeira
        where mountain firs comb water
from clouds after dusk

the *Levadeiro* cools warming
        tempers of farmers in drought.
Across the Atlantic

(on a coast by the Pacific)
        I cycle round a place of learning
in the lap of another mountain;

sail an avenue of palms
        traverse El Camino Real.
Here morning fog masks

silicon(e), dairy-free yoghurt
        politesse and privilege
and TV news breaks trill

of 'empty pool' parties
        to save a dry Cal. State.
Under vaulted windows

light rains
        down
on the pages of an adoptee citizen

(who walked with placards here
        who saw the Redwood bloom)
I drink songs of *quiet deputies*

sift bones of poems
        and dreams—
when evening comes

sleep rolls in like a blanket, stitched
        with a thousand precious needles
to comb this life from the day.

On finding and not finding Levertov

Northside, Valentines, on stone alcove seat, I sit with banana
peels and cigarettes, dark spirits in a plastic cup. Bluebottles
buzz over down and debris, sickly sweet, stale. I gaze across
the long-water, looking for pieces of you; try to glimpse your
reflection in this place in which you played, which played on
you, framed, shaped and held you; bridges made of shells,
grottoes of stone and sand.

Rococo: flint, limestone, ormer, conch

Here you 'saw with a double vision,' believed 'places
reveal' 'their longings,' 'inherent dreams' for 'something
more'. While others lived content behind 'grey curtains
of low expectation,' you saw the face of an imagined future,
envisioned departures   flecked by light of the moon.

Rococo: flint, limestone, ormer, conch

Two weeks before my arrival, the world watched a tower burn
in Kensington and Chelsea. Today in this old commuter town,
mosquitoes dwell at the Jacob's Well and rubbish rolls in the
streets; weeds embrace cracks out of sight, out of the eastern
part of Greater London once mapped as 'The Western Part
of the County of Essex in England.'

Rococo: flint, limestone, ormer, conch

How to look with child's eyes among forgotten children?
With eyes that saw 'thrones of Oberon and Titania' in
'two great stone seats'? And what was believed 'a Roman
road, though never authenticated as such'. Here by 'a well
under a lake where the muse moved,' (restored, but less
romantic / reduced but more complicated), I shut my eyes
to see.

Rococo: flint, limestone, ormer, conch

a girl in double
image
in a place she would no longer
recognize

Rococo: flint,   limestone,   ormer,   conch

each tiny fragment
flecked
reflecting moonlit waters

/ of her making.

Cedar tree

Today, I touched the cedar
tree as though to sense
a pulse; thread

a way through
a wooded past
unspool

exposure of you.
And though I felt
more than a thousand

years of life humming
there, in which you believed,
under which you cultivated

a life of Awe,
I could not
palpate the precise

pulse of your making. For
what matters
              is not
what is
     or how
         it was

but how you saw
it: iridescent
splash of goose

true soft grey
of dove. I try to photograph
the ancient expanse

of cedar bark
with my smart-
phone; but of course, no lens

can capture
the scale of all that
time;

all I'm left with
is a reduction,
                    or nothing

  resembling a path
                    to you
                        as a child in the timeless-numinous—
A view
            across the long water
                        (for which there is no 'i')

The Rilke Index

after Denise Levertov's personal index to the Selected Letters of Rainer Maria Rilke

'Autumn the creator'
(Index item #1)

True singing / is a *whispering*
(Rilke wrote) on autumn winds
perfection pressed
more creative
than even-toned spring.

It hums along the avenue
of original grief
polished as a stone.

And each of us—
particulate (borrowed, stolen, given, found)—
who *write long letters* every evening
for the chance of breathing

ride the amber highways of a song-   *piling sky—*

'Open secret'
(Index item #13/#13.5)

Safe in a womb
of twig held by branches,
the peltops sings her inwardness.
Her decorated temple
laid bare; a secret:

> that she makes no distinction
> *between her h/art*
> *and the world's.*

Perhaps one day you will 'let yourself
approach the mountain.'
Raise yourself to silvery
peaks, witness her song.

For there is only one
kind of desire
that takes this work further:

> The will 'to begin,
>> to be (to defy)'—

to advance step by step
toward a kind of living
sure of itself—

like a bird-note, gently caught
at the very edge of things.

The living / room
(After index items #29 and #35)

You call me and your need
erases me.
        I cannot hear
        my mind. Fractured,
        molecular, there is only dissipation.

But in the living room
             dust
will settle, ink
will set, signature
await the bow.
        Fingermarks
        against each fret
will gleam like quiet deputies.

In the living
room (place of turning,
             place of life) exhalations
will catch against pane
like a crime scene
        resisting
erasure.   Gathering
fine threads to *carry,*
        give birth,
             allow
each thing its own evolution.

Until: *thrust out*
(upon a plane / of thing-like
solitude)   is

a forming:
distinct (and singular)
as the dew.

Rambler

On the way in
  and on the way out

    I pass a new-age
    dog-walker:

forest-spirit, Filipa,
  face ashine with the hot bold shock

    of summer. Golden
    -toothed she guides

a ranging pack of seven hounds
  with a surety at home in Hainault

    country and Seven Kings. Fluorescent
    hi-tops, leopard skin

knickerbockers, tied at the knee;
  a crown of bandanaed platinum

    dreadlocked hair.
    Like some fabled piper

she leads; knows
  each by name, shape, shift

    breath and bark—
    walks invisible lines each day

like embodied poetry,
  rambling brambles

                wild strawberry
                        fording   hidden streams.

        They trust her with a depth
            beyond human language,

                    follow her through gate and hatch
                        trace tracks divined like an attuned mother.

        On the flats she stops, speaks
            to me of horses

                    [insider to outsider
                        familiar to gooseberry fool]:

        'newly enclosed they are
            but with no shade or water.'

                The lines
                    on her face

        deepen, in sudden loss
            of unconcern, as I listen without answer

                    on the tip of a stranger's tongue. In a breath, she disappears
                        into speckled light.

        If only I knew how to follow—
            to be   (dog-like)

                    pilgrim, traveler;   cast myself
                        from the flickering fine, fragile / *edge of the world*—

Lean of leg tramping
deep in dappled arpeggio

feral strawberry, blackberry thorn
wild gooseberry, in bloom—

The way there

Roll up
your sleeves.
Wrestle in the dust
of the common world.
Walk daily
among birds and multitudes;
taste wild mint and fruits.
Sit awhile
on an old stone
bench of conch and limestone; listen

with your eyes
          at the turn
of a chalk-lined creek
where the *reader*
          gets splashed with clear water.

Forming, transforming

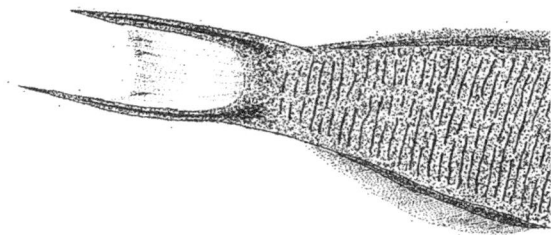

Sensitive

for Rilke

You dwelled in the longing
place. Felt yourself inside

a stone; a ray of light
the vastness of space—

and returned, always
to the daily task

of wonder. You
knew of harshness

but shunned
it. Listened

instead to early morning
sounds through a window:

> a cane on stone
> the flower woman

> that dog sifting through
> stirrings. You found

comfort in the great unseen
familiarity. Painted with your 'ear

as for the eye,' buzzing
in nearness of silence.

Your commitment

'nameless,' all encompassing:

Not merely to react
But to decide
Not merely to be formed
But to transform

To grow
into a decision—

to feel
the weft, the sit

of the cut, its warp unknown
against skin. Each fibre

stirring you to move toward
                        freedoms
to teach yourself
               to stride out—   (tentative, then eager)

            to feel sweet grass
            under each tender foot

                   and your bold
                   long bones, expanding—

Night vision

Step out from under scarcity
into shimmering night. Tender
flesh of courage unskinned, quivers
in breeze called hope. Open to embrace
of love unlanguaged, lingering, hidden
heart quietly beating in underbrush.

Gain night vision. Navigate thicket
of ambivalence and doubt. Track life
at the edge of breathing. A great chorus
peels above, presses at ear drums, rattles
tentative feet. Train grief-sharpened
sights to tender shoots. Seek

small hand waiting. Hold tight.

Axis of a shifting world, I

In winter light
each tree slides on an axis
to human eye invisible.

Toward the helix lookout
tiny birds, like moths
rest warm bodies

on tall grasses.
Each slender blade
bends in gesture of giving.

So many bodies
up here.
Heel-to-toe

I coax my own
round reedy hill
in walking meditation.

My hope: to catch
a glimpse
of what it is *to be*

(a small smooth body
bending
a blade of grass).

Axis of a shifting world, II

Lean into me.
Let me stand
where you can no longer.

Solitude surrounds us
of course, even 'two by two'
as we are in 'the ache of it'.

From this vantage
we glimpse
a kite
let it drag us
a way, kick off the dust.

Lean into me.
Around us is sky
and the remnants
of ritual.
        And you
and now you: the axis
is shifting.

Although it is possible
I had you in mind
all along you

are
rewriting
me. My maps
are re-charting.

Will you know me
when you
           become
and I am
           rewritten?

The one light is the light in all bodies

On a branch of downy birch
flecked with river light

two crows cool
their tongues, one

unseasonable London summer.
I walk along the heronry pond

toward the wild
centre; a tremolo of futures

enforced by Brisbane blue.
This is Wanstead

that drew us
over and over

into its basic poetry.
In its serpentine lake

we envisioned early music
among golden dead

leaves.   The past
snakes across parched beds today:

captured
            plastic chairs and bottles;

            the ruined
                        boathouse still

ghosted through trees. I water
in the shade

with two welcoming Sikhs
who speak of a runaway

trans-boy, lost,
somewhere by the River Roding.

The selfsame
tributary of this place

that held our heads
above water

when we thought we might / drown.
'By his auburn hair you'd know him,' they say

—without using those pronouns.

They feed a solitary duck

in the uncomfortable

heat.

In the silence
this inscribes (the emergent

space between)
I am untongued with erasures: *of you*

and so me; each baroque
note of a viol lowing

as soft strings
of new boy-hair

held   by water crowfoot—
                ekaa jot jot hai sareera.

One light: all bodies
gold as changing leaves.

Axis of a shifting world, III

I need to be in the world.
To feel
air, breath of lives
            (various). Faces —

not only on subways
more than *petals* —
wings
material, immaterial.
The movement
of limbs: mine
theirs; the flicker
of life on brows
            (various). Bustling women

with prams. Old
couples, touching
in their concern
still.
From there, of course, I think
of you. I think about
our intertwining
our changing
            (various, and particular)

so much that is strange
and new. Now
a plate of food:
yellow eggs
green kale

(your favourite)
the anticipation
of bitter
coffee
and times
         (various)
         with you.

Day begins with an/other line by Neruda, after reading Komunyakaa

I have been fertile in everything / that has happened to me, the sho
of my arrival, each fumbling creation of a child's hand through dus
-motes, shards of light, in corners of infinite silence. And later,
in cracks between the hurricanes of my body, strange snow
of my limbs. I have been fertile through loss of matriarch, of uncle,
hopes, selves, days of blood, your bursting through loam, the slow
work of change. I have been fertile on still mornings, in days of fog
of failure. I have been fertile in kitchen catastrophe, song sung,
foxtrot across cool tile.

There is germination in our whispers, love
those dreams of which we dream, the kind that lift like wedgetails
tracing thermals through the day. I have been fertile in gullies
greened by sluicing waters, faithful to each splicing of the heart
of place, the flooding of our fissures, grafting your spirit to vine.

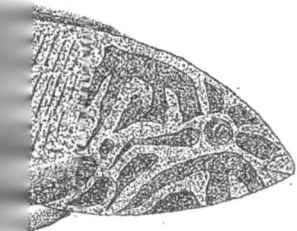

Arriving

Moon Wrasse

Here
    you are
    my Blue Moon
Wrasse
New-born
barely imagined being

I see you
with a new lucency—
clear as the blue
of your new man suit
               sweet as the sky
               true as day

Back and forth
you carve
this place of ours
continuing
a persistent insistence
on incessant activity—
you always loved
to dance
        some things change, some stay the same

Here
    you are
    forming, transforming
twinkling your webbed toes
shaking your tail
crescent. Lyre-wrasse

we cycle
through the dappled light
of the casuarina—
holding hands
like younger lovers
in a film
in a dream

All is calm and comfort
here, moving in
our translucent
cocoon
'self-made' and safe
as houses—
Or as a fresh-made pair
of parrot fish
pyjamas.

A promontory / A memory

*For the sake of a single verse, one must see many cities,
men and things; one must know the animals, one must
feel how the birds fly and know the gesture with which...
flowers open in the morning. One must be able to think back
to... mornings by the sea, to the sea itself...* Rainer Maria
Rilke, *The Notebooks of Malte Laurids Brigge.*

Pink and purple pig-face
   tailors of the coast
      salt-resistant sentries
         of *the sea itself.*

      Feathered faces rise
    caress each arc of blustering
  morning; a hundred tiny baskets
set on a ledge to catch the light.

Their gesture fills a space
   that *walks with me,*
   walks beside me,
      treads here too:

    a solitude like rain
   against the cheek
  of the heart. A daily bow,
overlooked, an unaccounted Volta

spun to song of sun
   played at waning moon. A
      motion so assured
         it knows of endings

and beginnings,
of animals, the flight of birds,
nocturnal stirrings that make a city's
fringe. Along a windswept ridge

(where emerald bauble, shallow root
stich the edge of the world),
we do the work of gathering,
saltwater, impressions pressed

—time, tide and memory—
against leaves of mind.
Each gesture is a promise
of a different quality;

gifts of turquoise beads
from *sleeve of sea*—

memorandum: floreat:

Watering wayward pots one morning
life returns—smaragdine—
from the carnage of a cold-hearted summer.
Nascent fronds reveal themselves
to an astonished, awakening eye.

So much *is* again
possible.

       I read everything
like a message in the moss
in a place where violets
persistently open
all along
       the *crumbling wall.*

The waiting gesture

I take into myself the origin / and laughter of the wate
through my wrists. / To drink would seem too much, to
obvious; / but with this quiet waiting-gesture comes / brigh
water flowing into my consciousness. Rainer Maria Rilke
Collected Works, vol iii.

With quiet waiting
   gesture, take water
      at your wrists. A constant

spring is here—has been
   here—even without you
      finding it. Now, lean to sip

with gentle hands (take care
   not to bruise the fruit). Palm
      over palm pass this gift

like a jewel: tending
   the shape—of something—
      forming. Gesture of giving,

continuum of gestures, (the real
   image, steps toward
      the actual): the clarity of gum

in winter. The shock of autumn
   on blue. Hold, still, listen
      at the crack where the world

starts speaking. Amid ferns
   and bracken, leaf litter
      at your feet. A paper wasp

in visitation drinks
at the wrist of your
submission. Then thought

is a splash like a sliver
of light
and all the day is words—

All of it

after Rilke's 'The Second Elegy'

Alone, s*uddenly alone*
  we *breathe ourselves*—
    suspended—

the heart, a corridor of light
  expands to embrace the morning.
    Silence, the calmest of hands, rests

on the shoulder
  until the leading *bird-note* reaches out across the ridge
    riding a shock of *rose-gold*

assured in its becoming.
  Today is a day like any other.
    How then, to hold in the palm of the mind

this dialectic jewel?
  It breaks the being open.
    Down below, the river

continues a patient carving
  and the counterfeit knowing you brought here
    is a skin

shed
  loose among leaf litter.
    Any step now

soft of fleshly foot
  through unfurling fern and bracken
    is a tender assertion of newness;

a translucent understanding
that this is all there is:
all of it:

an ecology of selves
(a kaleidoscope)
an extended ecstasy

of un-possession—

After Malouf *Flights, 3*

Our bodies are breakable. Supplicating themselves
　　　　　at the cliffs of our daily
　　　　　sorrows they smash, high
　　　　　and wide the waters of our thoughts.

Time stays silent.
Witness:

We are blinded. Folded.
We step
　　　in, step out.

We wait. We exhale
salt. It is bitter on our
tongue. We wait for
the next sweet moment.

We are monsoonal. Always
　　　　　threatening to break our horizons—

We pulse under our filamental
surface. We are spectacular
disruptions of tissue, explosions
of grape, cherry, grey, and the
yellow-green of our self-betrayal.

By the time we have
　　　　　our bearings—

our fields, scarred
and raked, studded
with half-shorn trunks

of where, who, what, everything,

everything,

we once thought—

we blink naked
to the clear-cracked
sky, to watch the arrival
of our true nature.

The last of this red hour

In the space
we inhabit
one burnished

afternoon, we sip
a taste of silence
from 'an autumn

of silences':
faithful and bright, full
of images and words

like skeletons of powder
hulks with crowns of mangrove hair.
As the golden hour

blooms, tinged with aubergine,
a shiver   along water-glass
almost breaks our spell. Each step

is incantation:
a stilt, a turn, a black swan pair
paddle poetry,

dreams. When the chorus warms
—arpeggios for the show—
of 'word bells' and wattle-birds

who know the pace of poem-time
who know the promise of afternoon
lines—   the ripple

of this light—
we fix to stay
forever; feather

our minds
with baubles
against a northern wall;

suspend our home
across a watercourse
catch forgotten

lines / 'break the skin
on the pool
of ourselves'

every sounding
afternoon. As the orchid sky
flies over, we

scribble birds
whispered words
in a tesserae of light;

that knows the pace of poem-time
that knows the promise of afternoon lines;

in the last of this red hour
in this cathedral of song.

Note to self (in Novel times)

Remember   to love
the world.   Love
the wailing,   rolling world;
the air;   the wildness
of wind   lifting a million kites
of change.

                Love
the deep,   challenging dark
of water;   the topography
                of spirit:
                        a wheatfield
                        a canyon
                        an undulating plateau;

that human   dream
of time   and space
lean into   *that,*
                and this:

the singular   note
of your human heart
calling,   calling
you home.

Acknowledgements

Poems in this collection were written on the unceded lands of the Wangal, Dharug and Gundungurra peoples. I pay my respects to Elders past and present, and to all First Nations Australians for their ongoing connection to place and the keeping of story.

This work was written with the support of a Macquarie University Research Training Pathways scholarship, an Australian Post Graduate Award, and two generous travel grants from Macquarie University. Development of the work was further assisted by the Australian Government through the Australia Council, its arts funding and advisory body.

Several of the poems in this collection have appeared in various journals and anthologies, often in earlier form. I give thanks to the editors of the following publications for their faith in my work:

'After Malouf *Flights, 3'* first appeared in *Cordite Poetry Review*, Issue 43.0: 'Masque,' 2013.

'Some words for migratory birds' first appeared in *Meniscus*, Volume 3, Issue 1, 2015.

'Propagules for drift and dispersal' first appeared in *Australian Poetry Anthology, 2015*.

'Seed' first appeared as 'This season's out-welling' in *Bukker Tillibul* #10, 'Hauntings Special Issue,' 2016, and subsequently in *Science Write Now*, Edition 6, 'Natural History and Historians,' 2022.

'Up to our knees in it' first appeared in *Bukker Tillibul* #10, 'Hauntings Special Issue,' 2016.

'Moon Wrasse' first appeared in *Writing from Below*, Volume Number 1. MASC. 2016.

'Note to self (in Novel times)' first appeared in 'the in/completene of human experience,' *TEXT* Volume 24.1 Special Issue 58, 2020, ar subsequently in *the incompleteness book*, Recent Work Press, 2020.

'The Levadiero' first appeared in *Plumwood Mountain Journal of Ecopoetry and Ecopoetics*, Volume 8, Number 1. 2021.

'The Rilke Index' first appeared in *TEXT* Volume 25, Issue special 6 *Poetry Now*, 2021.

'The last of this red hour' first appeared in *Science Write Now*, Edition 5, 'Illustration and Illumination,' 2021.

'memorandum: floreat:' first appeared in *StylusLit*, Issue 11, 2022.

'Night Vision' first appeared in *The Canberra Times*, 26th November 2022.

'The way there' first appeared in *AXON: Creative Explorations*, Volume 12.2 'Archives, counter-memory, creative practice and poetry,' 2022.

'On finding and not finding Levertov' first appeared in *AXON: Creative Explorations*, Volume 12.2 'Archives, counter-memory, creative practice and poetry,' 2022.

'Sail' was longlisted for the Grieve Writing Awards, 2021 and reprinted in *Grieve* Volume 10, 2022.

'Ways of seeing' placed second in the Tom Collins Poetry Prize, 2021.

74

'The one light is the light in all bodies' was shortlisted for the Val Vallis Award, 2022.

Gratitude to the judges of each of these prizes.

Sincere thanks to Marcelle Freiman for skilled supervision of the two research projects that birthed early versions of several of the poems in this collection. Immense gratitude to Felicity Plunkett for sensitive mentorship, attuned editorial guidance and artistic encouragement as I redeveloped the poems for general publication (you helped me believe, and for that I am forever in your debt). To Quinn Eades for publishing the title poem early on in the journey of this work, and for taking the time to read the full manuscript and offer such beautiful words for the cover all these years later. To Jill Jones for equally sensitive, generous reading and endorsement. To Adam Byatt for the gorgeous Moon Wrasse illustrations for the section dividers. And to my publisher David Musgrave, for believing in this collection and taking it on.

Finally, to Boden, for being my person. Always.

Notes

'Seed': 'what cannot be / is' alludes to Jennifer Moxley's claim that 'lyric utterances record voices structurally barred from social and political power' as 'what fails to be ... IS'. 'Lyric Poetry and the Inassimilable Life,' *The Poker*, 6 (2005).

The art of losing: section title is from Elizabeth Bishop's 'One Art'.

'Up to our knees in it': 'suddenly stops the breath' is from Mary Oliver's *A Poetry Handbook* (1994: 22).

'Propagules for drift and dispersal': this title is from Norman C. Duke's *Australia's Mangroves* (2006: 21); 'viviparous seeding habit' is from Richard Lear and Tom Turner's *Mangroves of Australia* (1977: 2); 'seeds... parents' is a variation on a line from K. Kathiresian's *Training Course on Mangroves and Biodiversity, Module 3.4* 'Biology of Mangroves' (139); 'drowned river valley' is from Duke (2006: 69); 'sentence based rehearsal' is from Andy Clark's 'Language: The Ultimate Artifact,' *Being There* (1998: 209); 'the mangrove... families in the world' is from Lear and Turner (1997: 2).

'The children': this poem responds to, and makes use of the following words from Vera Newsom's 'Sligo': 'children', 'trees', 'bird[s]', 'hurtl[ing]', 'electric', 'river', 'voices', 'glass', 'geometry', 'stone houses', 'roofs'.

'Sail': 'crack in the world', 'wailing', 'wind' are from *Selected Letters of Rainer Maria Rilke 1902-1926* (Trans. R.F.C. Hull 1946: 173); 'desolate', 'wind', 'sweep my knowledge', 'into oblivion', 'drop me back in the well' are from Denise Levertov's 'Desolate Light,' *Candles in Babylon* (1982).

'Archaeology': 'The archaeology of grief' is from Helen Macdonald's *H is for Hawk* (2014: 199); 'forgotten ways of sight' is an allusion to a phrase from the same passage; 'silver moon not yet lost / at bottom of silted well' is an allusion to a line from Denise Levertov's 'Everything that Acts Is Actual,' *Here and Now* (1957); 'weigh' and 'by... carat of... heart' are from *Letters of Rainer Maria Rilke Vol II, 1910-1926*, (Trans. Greene & Norton 1948: 297); 'blood', 'glance and gesture' are from Rainer Maria Rilke's *The Notebooks of Malte Laurids Brigge* (Trans. Norton 1949: 27).

On finding and not finding Levertov: section title refers to the poet Denise Levertov, 1923-1997. The epigraph is from her 1973 essay collection *The Poet in the World* (114).

'The Levadeiro': the *Levadeiro* is responsible for the control and rotation of irrigation water through the historic network of the *Madeira Levadas*; 'quiet deputies' is from *Selected Letters of Rainer Maria Rilke 1902-1926* (Trans. Hull 1946: 402), the passage was indexed by Denise Levertov in her personal edition of the letters.

'On finding and not finding Levertov': 'Valentines' refers to Valentines Mansion, Valentines Park, Ilford, UK. The once derelict mansion and surrounding landscaped gardens was a childhood place significant to Denise Levertov's imaginary and appears in her work throughout her career; 'saw with a double vision', 'places reveal', 'their longings', 'inherent dreams', 'something more' are from 'Something More,' *Sands of the Well* (1996); 'face of an imagined future' is an allusion to 'The Well,' *Breathing the Water* (1987); 'departure[s]' is from 'The Stricken Children,' *Breathing the Water* (1987); 'The Western Part of the County of Essex in England' is from 'A Map of the Western Part of the County of Essex in England,' *The Jacobs Ladder* (1961); 'thrones of Oberon and Titania', 'two great stone seats' and 'what was [believed] a Roman road though never authenticated as such' are from 'The Sense of Pilgrimage' (1967), reprinted in *The Poet in the World* (1973: 75); 'A well / under [a] lake where the muse move[d]' is from 'The Illustration,' *The Jacob's Ladder* (1961); 'I shut my eyes to see' is an allusion to a line from an unpublished manuscript of Levertov's c.1960 (Stanford University Libraries M0601, Series 2, Box 22, Folder 43); *The Double Image* was the title of Levertov's first poetry collection (published under Levertoff, 1946).

'Cedar tree': this cedar tree, situated in Valentines Park and still standing today, was at the time of Levertov's childhood 'reputed to be 1,000 years old' (Levertov 'The Sense of Pilgrimage,' 1967, reprinted in *The Poet in the World* 1973: 75).

'The Rilke Index': poems in this sequence are a synthesis of response, citation and allusion. Poem titles in inverted commas are taken verbatim from Levertov's personal index labels to *Selected Letters of Rainer Maria Rilke 1902-1926* (Trans. R.F.C. Hull 1946). The index provided significant cognitive scaffolding to Levertov's poetics. Where possible, substantive material from Rilke is indicated by the use of italics, and substantive material from Levertov (or others) is indicated by the use of inverted commas. Smaller usages and allusions are generally not marked, but noted below.

'Autumn the creator': this title was Levertov's index label for the following passage from Rilke's letters: '... I want the autumn! It almost seems as if autumn were the true creator, more creative than the spring, which is too even toned... This great, splendid wind piling sky upon sky—I would like to go into its country and along its highways' (Trans. Hull 1946: 74). The entry was the first in her 'Rilke Index'; 'True singing is', 'whispering' are from Rilke's 'Third Sonnet of Part 1,' *Sonnets to Orpheus* (Trans. Stephen Cohn 2000); 'perfection pressed' and 'write long letters' are from, and 'hums along the avenue' is an allusion to, Rilke's 'Herbsttag' (Autumn Day) *The Book of Images,* quoted by Hull in *Selected Letters* in a note on the page indexed by Levertov as 'Autumn the creator', see title note; 'more creative / than', 'even toned', spring' are from Rilke, from the indexed passage; 'original grief / polished as a stone' is a synthesis of a line from Rilke's 'Elegy 10,' *Duino Elegies* (Trans. Martyn Crucefix, *AGENDA*

Vol 42 Nos. 3-4, Spring 2007: 123) and a line from Levertov's 'Fear of the Blind,' *The Collected Poems of Denise Levertov* (2013: 7); 'piling sky' is from Rilke, from the indexed passage.

'Open secret': this title was Levertov's index label (item #13.5) for the following passage from Rilke: 'But this is not the place to speak of our experiences; they are secret, not a secret that locks itself up, not one that demands to be kept hidden, it is a secret that is sure of itself, that stands open like a temple whose portals exult in being portals and whose towering pillars sing that they are the gateway' (1946: 266). Levertov listed this entry adjacent to the entry entitled 'Pollen' (item #13), a label pointing to two passages (cited below) that bookend the following: '...in the sense of the "open secret" of Nature' (1946: 240). Levertov herself published two poems entitled 'Open Secret,' in *Relearning the Alphabet* and *Evening Train* (1970; 1992); 'womb'; 'sing'; 'inwardness'; 'that she makes no distinction / between her h/art / and the world's' are from a letter from Rilke to Lou Andreas-Salomé, '...the bird on this inward journey: her nest is practically an external womb granted to her by nature... Thus she is the one creature to have a very special kind of feeling of trust in the external world, as though she knew herself to be in harmony with its most intimate secrets. That is why she sings in it as if singing her own inwardness, that is why we receive a bird-note so easily into our depths... for a moment it turns our whole world into an interior landscape, because we feel the bird does not distinguish between her heart and the world's' (Trans. Hull 1946: 238). The letter was indexed by Levertov as 'Pollen', see title note, and final note, below; 'temple' and 'secret' are from the passage indexed as 'Open secret'; 'let [yourself] / approach the mountain' and 'silvery' are from Levertov's 'Open Secret', *Evening Train* (1992); 'takes this work further' alludes to Levertov's index title 'Further than Work' for the following passage from Rilke: 'For much as the artist in us is concerned with <u>work</u>, the realization of it, its existence and duration quite apart from ourselves – we shall only be wholly in the right when we understand that even this most urgent realization of

a higher reality appears, from some last and extreme vantage-poir
only as a means to win something once more invisible, somethii
entirely inward and unspectacular, – a saner state in the midst of o
being' (Trans. Hull 1946: 330). Levertov also indexed the passa
a second time as 'Life and Death'; 'to begin, / to be (to defy) –'
from, and 'toward a kind of living' alludes to, Levertov's 'Beyon
The End,' *Here and Now* (1957); 'sure of itself' and 'bird-note' ar
from the passage indexed as 'Open secret'; 'the very edge of things'
an allusion to the following line from Rilke, indexed by Levertov a
'Pollen': 'In place of anything coherent I shall only write down on
or two notes just as they come to me during my reading, all pointin
beyond the edge of the *Letters*, at us, at me' (Trans. Hull 1946: 238).

'The living / room': 'Fingermarks' is an allusion to the followin;
line from Martyn Crucefix: '...the fingerprints of two very differen
worlds lie all over these great poems,' *AGENDA* Vol. 42, Nos. 3-4
Spring 2007 (116); 'quiet deputies' is from the following passage from
Rilke's letters: '...the "I" was only the first and last stimulus, but...
from then on remains facing you... thrust out... so far upon the plane
of artistic engagement, of thing-like solitude, that you feel yourself
sharing in the completion of this mysterious object like some quiet
deputy' (1946: 402). This passage comes from a longer section of
text underlined by Levertov and indexed twice, as both 'Subjectivity'
(index item #29) and 'Initiation into the mysteries of Poetry' (index
item #35); 'turning' is from Rilke: 'the turning that *must* come if I
am to live...' (Trans. Hull 1946: 243, italics in original); 'exhalations'
is from Rilke (Trans. Hull 1946: 402); 'carry', 'give birth', 'allow each
thing its own evolution' are from Rilke's *Letters to a Young Poet* (Trans.
Cohn 2000, qtd by Crucefix 2007: 117); 'thrust out', 'upon [a] plane',
'of thing-like / solitude' are from Rilke, from the indexed passage.

'Rambler': 'Filipa', 'Hainault', 'Seven Kings' are from Denise Levertov's
'A Map of the Western Part of the County of Essex in England,' *The
Jacob's Ladder* (1961); 'gooseberry fool' is from *Selected Letters of
Rainer Maria Rilke 1902-1926* (Trans. Hull 1946); 'edge of the world'

is from Levertov's 'The Poet Li Po Admiring a Waterfall,' *Life in the Forest* (1978).

'The way there': 'Roll up / your sleeves' is a variation on a line from, and 'wrestle' and 'dust of the common world' are from, Ralph J. Mills Jr. on Denise Levertov, *Poets in Progress*, (1967: 210); 'where the reader / gets splashed with [clear] water' is from Henri Cole in 'The Art of Poetry, No. 98, Henri Cole, interviewed by Sasha Weiss,' *The Paris Review*, Issue 209, Summer 2014.

Forming, transforming: section title is from Denise Levertov's 'Web,' *A Door in the Hive* (1989).

'Sensitive': 'a stone' is from Rilke's 'Erinnerung' (Memory), *Selected Poems* (Trans. MacIntyre 1940); 'space', 'harshness' is from Rilke's 'Before the Spring,' in 'Six translations of Rilke: Stephen Cohn,' *AGENDA* Vol 42. Nos. 3-4, Spring 2007 (27); 'a cane on stone / the flower woman / that dog sifting through / stirrings' is an allusion to a passage from *Selected Letters of Rainer Maria Rilke 1902-1926* (Trans. Hull 1946: 141-2). The passage was indexed by Levertov as 'Sounds in the Night'; 'ear is for the eye' is from the same Rilke passage; 'buzzing in the nearness /of silence' alludes to a passage from Rilke's letters indexed by Levertov as 'Bees of the Invisible' (Trans. Hull 1946: 394); 'commitment', 'nameless' are from Rilke's 'Duino Elegies IX,' quoted in 'Translations of Rilke and a commentary: W.D. Jackson,' *AGENDA* Vol 42. Nos. 3-4, Spring 2007 (66); 'Not merely to react… transform' is from W. D. Jackson on Rilke, in the same essay (66).

'Axis of a shifting world, II': 'Lean into', 'solitude', 'a kite', 'drag', 'sky', 'ritual' are from Levertov's 'Spring in the Lowlands,' *Overland to the Islands* (1958); 'two by two', 'the ache of it' are from Levertov's 'The Ache of Marriage,' *O Taste and See* (1964).

'The one light is the light in all bodies': gender pronouns might be seen as the language frontier of our time. As a partner to a transgender person, one is acutely attuned to this threshold, and to the profound pain of erasure caused by the frequent missteps around it in the form of misgendering, even when unintentional. Due to our enmeshment in colonial capitalism and its insistence on the cis gender binary, almost everybody struggles with pronouns beyond this framework at first—even progressives, even queers, even people as inclusive and (in my experience) generally open-hearted as people of the Sikh faith—as re-learning, like love, like any form of care, always entails *work*. Language matters. Pronouns matter. Misgendering harms us all. The tragedy of this particular encounter was a failure of language in the sense of a failure of knowing, but it was subsequently a failure on my part to speak up as an ally. This poem seeks to restore what I was unable to restore in this particular moment, 'un-tongued' as I was by a symbolic collision of approaches to in/visibility, bodily identity signification, 'passing', and issues of other/ing and erasure in their many forms and histories.

'drew [us,] over and over into its basic poetry, / in its serpentine lake' is from Denise Levertov's 'A Map of the Western Part of the County of Essex in England,' *The Jacob's Ladder* (1961); 'among golden dead / leaves' and 'that held our heads / above water / when we thought we might / drown' are variations on lines from, and 'envisioned early music', 'ghosted through trees' and 'viol' are allusions to, the same poem; 'ekaa jot jot hai sareera' ('The One Light is the light in all bodies') is from the *Guru Granth Sahib* - 'Ang 125'; the poem recounts an encounter in the place of Levertov's 'Map'.

'Axis of a shifting world, III': 'subways... petals' is an allusion to Ezra Pound's 'In a Station of the Metro'.

'Day begins with an/other line by Neruda after reading Komunyakaa': this title refers to Yusef Komunyakaa's 'Nighttime Begins with a Line by Pablo Neruda,' which makes use of a line and several images from Pablo Neruda's 'The Human Condition'; 'I have been fertile in everything / that has happened to me', 'hurricanes' and 'snow' are from the same Neruda poem.

'Moon Wrasse': the Moon Wrasse (*Thalassoma lunare*), also known as the Blue Wrasse, Crescent Wrasse and Lyretail Wrasse, among other names, undergoes a female-to-male (FTM) transition in mid-life, a characteristic shared with the Parrot Fish. Italicised lines are from Caspar Henderson's *The Book of Barely Imagined Beings* (2013), Meg Keene's 'Hymn to Her,' recorded by The Pretenders, *Get Close*, Warner Music, CD, LP, (1986), and Denise Levertov's 'Web,' *A Door in the Hive* (1989) respectively; 'self-made' refers to a term of gender affirmation sometimes used within the FTM transgender community, short for 'self-made man'; 'pyjamas' is from 'Parrot Fish,' *National Geographic*.

'memorandum: floreat': 'violets... the crumbling wall' is a variation on a line from Denise Levertov's 'The Bereaved,' *Overland to the Islands* (1958).

'A promontory / A memory': epigraph is from Rilke's *The Notebooks of Malte Laurids Brigge* (Trans. M.D Herter Norton 1949/1992: 26); 'walks with me, / walks beside me' is from Denise Levertov's 'A Solitude' *The Jacobs Ladder* (1961); 'solitude like rain' is from Rilke's 'Solitude,' *Selected Poems* (Trans. C.F. MacIntyre 1940); 'impressions' is from *Selected Letters of Rainer Maria Rilke 1902-1926* (Trans. R.F.C. Hull 1946: 122-3); 'pressed' and 'against leaves of mind' allude to a line from Levertov: 'pressed between the mind's pages,' from 'It is here & now that matter most' (unpublished, Stanford University Library M0601, Series 2, Box 1 f44); 'sleeve of sea' is a variation on a line from Levertov's 'Fear of the Blind,' *The Collected Poems of Denise Levertov* (2013: 7).

'The waiting gesture': epigraph is from Rilke, quoted in a note by R.F.C. Hull in *Selected Letters of Rainer Maria Rilke 1902-1926* (1946: 191); 'gesture of giving' is an allusion to Denise Levertov's

'The Rights' *Here and Now* (1957), and also to the fact that Leverto indexed multiple pages from *Selected Letters of Rainer Maria Rilk 1902-1926* (Trans. Hull 1946) under the label 'Gestures', including th page containing the material in the epigraph cited above. The concep was significant to her understanding of creativity; 'continuum o gestures' is from Mary Oliver's *Winter Hours* (2000: 93); 'the rea image' is from Denise Levertov's 'Too easy: to Write of Miracles,' *Th Collected Poems of Denise Levertov* (2013: 9).

'All of it': 'suddenly alone', 'breathe ourselves', 'corridor', light' ar from Rilke's 'The Second Elegy' (Trans. Mitchell 2009); 'calmest of hands rests / upon the shoulder' is an allusion to a line from Rilke' 'The Second Elegy' as quoted in a note by Hull, *Selected Letters of Rainer Maria Rilke 1902-1926* (1946: 191); 'bird-note' is from Rilke. *Selected Letters* (Trans. Hull 1946: 283); 'rose-gold' is an allusion to Denise Levertov's 'Courage,' *Here and Now* (1957) and Rilke's 'The Second Elegy' (Trans. Mitchell 2009).

'After Malouf *Flights, 3*': 'Our bodies are breakable' is from, and 'arrival / of our true nature' is a variation on a line (from the same couplet) from David Malouf's 'Flights,' *Typewriter Music* (2007).

'The last of this red hour': 'an autumn of', 'silences' and 'faithful' are from Levertov's 'Everything that Acts is Actual,' *Here and Now* (1957); 'powder hulks' refers to the shipwrecks at Sydney's Homebush Bay and is an allusion to Robert Adamson's 'Powder Hulk Bay'; 'word bells' is from Patricia McCarthy's sequence 'Word Bells. From Rilke's Letters,' *AGENDA* Vol 42. Nos. 3-4, Spring 2007 (195-204); 'break the skin / on the pool / of ourselves' is from Seamus Heaney's 'Feeling into Words,' *Preoccupations: Selected Prose, 1968-1978* (1980: 47).

'Note to self (in Novel times)': poem written in March 2020; 'love / the world' is from Mary Oliver's 'To Begin With, the Sweet Grass,' *Evidence* (2009).